STATES OF MIND

I FEEL IMPATIENT

BY STEPHANIE FINNE

BLUE OWL BOOKS

TIPS FOR CAREGIVERS

Social and emotional learning (SEL) helps children manage emotions, create and achieve goals, maintain relationships, learn how to feel empathy, and make good decisions. The SEL approach will help children establish positive habits in communication, cooperation, and decision-making. By incorporating SEL in early reading, children will be better equipped to build confidence and foster positive peer networks.

BEFORE READING

Talk to the reader about what impatience is and what some potential triggers are.

Discuss: What is impatience? What can cause this feeling?

AFTER READING

Talk to the reader about what impatience feels like. Ask how the reader knows when he or she is feeling impatient.

Discuss: What do you feel in your body when you are impatient? What actions does it make you take? How can you manage your impatience?

SEL GOAL

Some students may struggle with impatience because they have a hard time controlling impulses. They may not be able to successfully consider their safety, respect for others, and appropriate social norms. Help readers develop decision-making skills. Help them learn to stop and think about their actions. How can they identify their options? What do they need to do to control their impulses? How can they reflect on their choices? Discuss how learning to do these things can help them make good decisions in the future.

TABLE OF CONTENTS

CHAPTER 1

WHAT IS IMPATIENCE?

Is it hard to wait in line? What about waiting for your birthday? Do you get grouchy when things don't happen when you want them to?

Impatience is feeling upset because you have to wait. You can also feel it when you are rushed. When that feeling lasts longer than a few seconds, it is a **mood**.

When you are impatient, you may feel **restless**, angry, or **anxious**. Jada and her sister have to take turns playing a new computer game. Jada has a hard time waiting. She gets restless and angry. She is feeling impatient.

LIMIT SCREEN TIME

The internet, TV, and video games entertain us instantly. This makes it difficult to enjoy things that take longer. Limit your screen time. This will help you be **patient**.

Milo's homework is taking longer than he wanted it to. He clenches his fists and starts breathing fast. His stomach gets upset.

Milo tries to be **mindful** and curious about his feelings. He notices the **sensations** in his body. He takes a break to get up and move around. He takes some deep breaths.

DEEP BREATHING

Try to relax by focusing on your breath. Breathe in. Imagine your breath is filled with calm. Breathe out. Imagine **stress** leaving your body with each breath.

CHAPTER 2

CAUSES OF IMPATIENCE

What causes impatience? One **trigger** could be when you have to wait. Joel becomes impatient when his teacher says no talking in class. He is **eager** to share his ideas with his friends.

You can lose patience when someone breaks a promise. Hannah's parents are divorced. Her mom is late to pick her up for a visit. Hannah begins to feel impatient.

You can feel impatient when a **goal** is out of reach. Charlie really wants to read the next book in his favorite series. But it isn't available at the library yet. He gets impatient.

This is a time when being impatient can be good. Why? Charlie's body and mind are telling him that reading is important to him!

Impatience affects those around you, too. Alexa is helping Kevin with an art project. Kevin isn't happy with his drawing. He gets **frustrated**. Alexa was only trying to help. She feels hurt.

PRACTICE EMPATHY

Try to practice **empathy**. If someone is frustrating you, take a moment to imagine yourself in his or her shoes. Why might he or she be acting this way?

CHAPTER 3

WORKING THROUGH IMPATIENCE

How can you work through feelings of impatience? The first step is to **identify** the feeling. What is happening in your mind and body?

Step two is to list your triggers. What makes you impatient? Think about the last time you felt this way. What caused it?

Step three is to try to calm yourself. Step away from the situation. Take slow, deep breaths. Picture somewhere you feel safe, happy, and loved. This can help you relax and have more patience while you wait.

CARE FOR YOUR BODY

When you are not well rested or getting the right **nutrients**, you can become frustrated easily. Be sure to get enough food, water, and sleep.

The last step is to make a mindful decision about what to do next. You might try to accept that your feeling may not change. Or maybe you try to change your thoughts about the situation. Another option is to do something else while you wait.

Being impatient is not fun. But the mood won't last forever. The more mindful you are of your triggers, the better you will be able to handle your impatience.

GOALS AND TOOLS

GROW WITH GOALS

Everyone feels impatient sometimes. There are ways to help control this mood.

Goal: Identify your triggers. Write down what makes you impatient. This will help you be prepared the next time you face a trigger.

Goal: Practice empathy. Imagine someone who has frustrated you in the past. Now, imagine what he or she might have been experiencing at the time.

Goal: Plan ahead. Think of things you can do the next time you feel impatient. Make a list of ways to calm yourself.

TRY THIS!

Try body mapping. Draw an outline of your body. Now think of all the places that feel different or sore when you are impatient. Your hands may clench. Your heart may beat fast. Color those places red. When these places start to feel red, you are feeling impatient. Talk to an adult you trust and make a plan for what to do when you start to feel red.

GLOSSARY

anxious
Worried or very eager to do something.

eager
Having or showing a lot of interest and excitement.

empathy
The ability to understand and be sensitive to the thoughts and feelings of others.

frustrated
Annoyed or angry.

goal
Something you aim to do.

identify
To recognize or tell what something or who someone is.

impatience
The state of being restless, not willing to wait, or easily annoyed.

mindful
A mentality achieved by focusing on the present moment and calmly recognizing and accepting your feelings, thoughts, and sensations.

mood
An emotion that lasts longer than a few minutes.

nutrients
Substances, such as proteins, minerals, or vitamins, that our bodies need to stay healthy.

patient
Able to put up with problems or delays without getting angry or upset.

restless
Unable to relax or be still because of excitement, anxiety, or boredom.

sensations
Particular feelings that your body experiences.

stress
Mental or emotional strain or pressure.

trigger
Something that causes an action or emotion.

TO LEARN MORE

FACT SURFER

Finding more information is as easy as 1, 2, 3.

1. Go to www.factsurfer.com
2. Enter "**Ifeelimpatient**" into the search box.
3. Choose your book to see a list of websites.

INDEX

Blue Owl Books are published by Jump!, 5357 Penn Avenue South, Minneapolis, MN 55419, www.jumplibrary.com

Library of Congress Cataloging-in-Publication Data

Names: Finne, Stephanie, author.
Title: I feel impatient / by Stephanie Finne.
Description: Minneapolis: Jump!, Inc., 2022.
Series: States of mind | Includes index. | Audience: Ages 7–10
Identifiers: LCCN 2020048937 (print)
LCCN 2020048938 (ebook)
ISBN 9781636901053 (hardcover)
ISBN 9781636901060 (paperback)
ISBN 9781636901077 (ebook)
Subjects: LCSH: Patience—Juvenile literature.
Classification: LCC BJ1533.P3 F56 2022 (print) | LCC BJ1533.P3 (ebook) | DDC 179/.9—dc23
LC record available at https://lccn.loc.gov/2020048937
LC ebook record available at https://lccn.loc.gov/2020048938

Editor: Eliza Leahy
Designer: Michelle Sonnek

Photo Credits: ladybirdstudio/Shutterstock, cover; Krakenimages.com/Shutterstock, 1, 5; Kamira/Shutterstock, 3; Sergey Novikov/Shutterstock, 4; Sam Wordley/Shutterstock, 6–7; Din Mohd Yaman/Shutterstock, 8–9; princessdlaf/iStock, 10; FatCamera/iStock, 11; fstop123/iStock, 12–13; Imcsike/Shutterstock, 14–15; liza54500/Shutterstock, 16; Goads Agency/iStock, 17; LightField Studios/Shutterstock, 18–19; seamind224/Shutterstock, 20–21.

Printed in the United States of America at Corporate Graphics in North Mankato, Minnesota.